# RUMOR

pimone triplett

# Rumor

poems

TriQuarterly Books
Northwestern University Press
Evanston, Illinois

TriQuarterly Books
Northwestern University Press
www.nupress.northwestern.edu

Printed in the United States of America

10  9  8  7  6  5  4  3  2  1

Library of Congress Cataloging-in-Publication Data

Triplett, Pimone.
    Rumor : poems / Pimone Triplett.
      p. cm.
    ISBN 978-0-8101-2628-2 (pbk. : alk. paper)
    I. Title.
    PS3570.R543R86 2009
    811.54—dc22

                                 2009024596

*Because of Lukas*

. . . nothing that happens, whether here on earth
or in the heavens or the seas below,
is missed by Rumor as she sweeps the world.

—Ovid

# contents

# Rumor

# When Rumor Itself

steps into

your garden,

the rock path lets go
its ruckus.

The carp-crowded water begs off.

A scrimmage of box hedge frays the finale,

all to keep the king waiting, licking

along the way          leaf spines

laurel spikes.

A fan of flames, vincula.

Something falls foul of the city,
clatters full out of the fracas,

turns us on as "old-fashioned
howitzers hitting bone."

She can shot-put the shadows at the center of his kingdom.

She can give or take a few faces of lesser gods.

He can hear the orchid's teeth grind beneath her sandal.

Sputters up, she,

several fables concerning

her offspring, church and state.

Begetting of which there was at first
a single word and its traces.

Crushes another, he,
thin-skinned iris.
Veins signatured.
Embryo's scalp.
Brain threads starting
to show through.

By which there is what happened
followed by the ghost of what happened.

Fight stink of new blood, wet steel.

When she jumps up, sends
her kids, spavin, tumbling in gutturals
all down the garden path,

she says          fire now,
and he does       from the guns

at his back. *Perfect*, she mutters.

He hits one pear blossom and it falls.

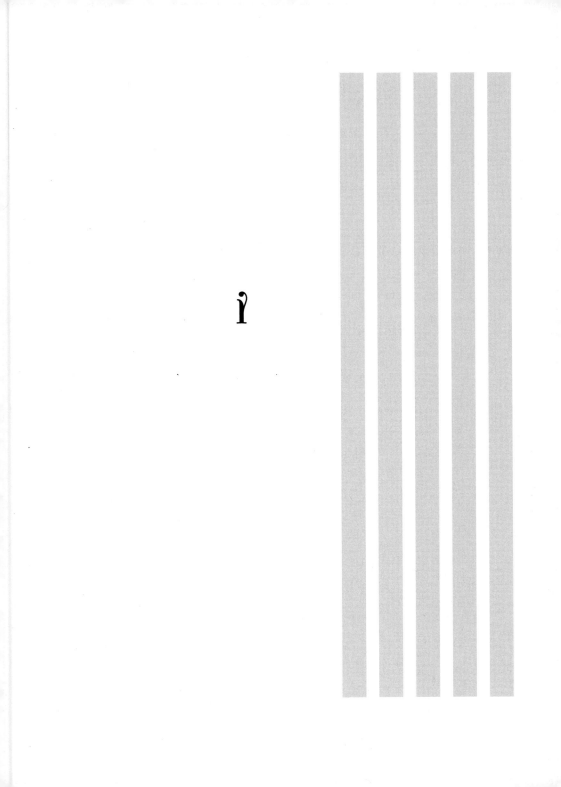

## Family Spirits, with Voice of One Child Miscarried

*(Thailand)*

Come in. Everyone does. This is the house of our name,
a tourist destination. Here, the legendary general,
  father-spawn, travels forever
   his flame of fluorescents
    and burning incense. Also we've got the World

  Bank posters for sale, servants humming
to pop tunes atonal, suffering the street's
  traffic blather. We've got boas
   below the driveway.
    A blue coral in the toilet bowl.

  As for the others,
the blind- and sunbeam,
  the pipe- and whip-snake,
   the dog-eared or dwarf—
    when someone rattles at a lily's foot, we listen.

*Oh but you can't be*      *always, you see, in residence,*

*can't hide behind the fence*      *of your city forever.*

*Why should more souls come*      *down, in sum, in sever,*

*be whomsoever*      *accident makes of skin?*

  Child, our sleep is your dream
danced open each morning by the girls
  selling fruit and rice.

There's a spank
               of hammers on tin, a clank of constant

construction,
sprouting capillary action,
        heavy electrical veins.
               Born into the trade, for money and motive we love
                       anyone long time, each of us all together.


*To be poured over*                    *the stone, for the repose*

*of flesh and its closed*              *riddles? But not to give,*

*as if wrong, a stroke*                *of soul, joke that still lives*

*like a fugitive,*                     *spirit thus being broken.*


        Built by a man in love
with change, this house of our name.
        Yesterday the seer, the one with the hole, the mole,
               on his face, told us how grandfather comes
                       back to this place often. He sits in the gold-flecked

pagoda, picking beige leaves from the money tree, eating
one apple after another. Planned the fall of a king, ruled this city
by charging for water. In this family we sigh,
        if only he'd been corrupt,
               we could have been really rich.


*Please, give more detail.*           *Things sexual come mostly*

*unclear. Who's the host,*            *what's below wet groundswell?*

*This taste of salt is*               *a business. Say you sell*

*the heart on fare-thee-wells.*       *Then best is not to be born.*


8

But also there is kindness. My cousin
carries the torch
　　　at our grandfather's cremation, bowing
　　　　　in uniform, jaw braced above his bright gold
　　　　　　　buttons, head bent, fingers splayed.

Later he commands all
paper flowers thrown
　　　into the fire. Here's yours.
　　　　　Let it go. The smoke alone helps the spirit
　　　　　　　to rise.

Coming back
with ashes in his hands, later he tells us
　　　because of the scent
　　　　　of burning body and his love
　　　　　　　he'll never eat bread again.

　　　　*Shadow falls on rock.*　　　　　*Aftershock. Refusal.*

　　　　*There's the first canal,*　　　　*birth and the other than.*

　　　　*If unborn, the stain*　　　　　*can remain so within,*

　　　　*so wedded to thin*　　　　　　*shadow it still goes to speak—*

Child, I don't know how else
to get at this. Goes the rumor, this life,
　　　a space-for-rent, as we own a corner of land
　　　　　that used to be slum, that's called the place
　　　　　　　of snakes. As for this being poured into

space, name, body, the era someone oh
so subtly plots you unto, maybe it's
　　　side-winding, maybe it's serpent. The skin
　　　　　comes off. Once I stood by a river watching
　　　　　　　the skin come off. Membrane of how

we wanted you, which was not enough
to keep you from turning back.
    Behind, along the path the snake had come,
        dirt, combed loosely,
                showing its tracks for a while.

# The Rumor of Necessity

*(Pattani, Thailand, and elsewhere)*

1

Again in the hotel of the head
                waters, it's all about
        the bird's nest soup.

Step one for the ancient elixir:
                boil one bird's nest, some rich stock, dry
        sherry, add egg whites to get this age-old

cure for impotence, which also brings
                long life. These days
        fifty of the half-teacup sculptures,

glued with swift work
                and saliva,
        can fetch a couple of K

on the open market. You can go there to see them
                as I have, spot where the winged
        architects shoot back and forth

inside a brick skull built near the river's
                beginnings,
        spitballing their one thought

of home. Watch boys and men by the dozens,
                for pennies a day,
        shinny up the walls,

hammer and chisel strapped to their

        slender limbs.
    Each species willing to do

what it takes. First the male then the female

        flies back to the empty
    ledge. In hot water, the nests separate

into long chewy strands.

        You can garnish with green onions
    and ham.

## 2

Meanwhile the head of state

        stating there has to be
    a firm hand, until

down the road everyone wants to know

        who the heroes are, who the villains are.
    And maybe you read the one about two boys arrested

from a village with no name. Or pictured the police rushing

        in, the boys suspected of dealing,
    coming as they did from the triangle of dirt

that starts behind our hotel

        where once upon a people
    poppies were the cure. There must be

a firm hand. The boys forced

        into "detox," then shoved down into
    the ground still alive.

Later someone in charge starts to think

        and we can parse that too,
    the winged

synapse flying back and forth

                  inside his skull to build
        the bright idea:

pouring onto their heads the hot coals

                and ashes, the urine
        and boiling soup.

Next day my mother

                closed the paper,
        drove us to a temple

where midday sun splits the gold

                face of the god she believes in
        practically in half. Outside, sounds of brake

squeals out on Mass Ave,

                kids below us counting *nung, song,*
        *sam, see,* the same

words she once taught me. We bent down to lay our heads

                against the green acrylic
        carpet's little circle round the shrine,

said our prayers for the one boy who survived.

                After weeks in the hospital
        it's the feet that can't be mended,

the skin shorn so cleanly off. I'm not saying

                in that building
        we were heard. Back in the homeland

the birds in motion, attracted by music,

                attracted by light.
        If you stand still you can hear them

ready to migrate, centuries of laying in caves given
                              up on. And when twilight arrives through
                    the phone-book thicknesses

of open slits in the hotel walls, you get their
                              slice in air,
                    scissor-sharp wings at full

dart and glide, their coming and going,
                              if you can make it out,
                    like pages shifted in wind, echo and shriek

over eons shaping their talent to eat
                              a single mosquito
                    in flight. There's the long buildup,

there's the boy who didn't make it. I'm related
                              to the heroes, related to the villains.
                    I want to give you the firm hand. Thrust it out now

for you to take, every hour, every harvest, with the hundred-wide
                              blade-on-a-whetstone
                    bird scream going up.

# Bodies, *the Exhibition*, Last Day with Ancient Sayings

Study grips the skin again, breaks it, prime
mover muscles removed, re-flexing the flesh
for these specimens, never claimed, about
to be contained in containers. The trucks idle.

Dissection demands the flayed-at-four-points
turkey-joint tendons, resin entering
the wrists by "forced impregnation." It's said,
*crows everywhere are equally black.*

As once upon a right deltoid, the knife
sliced clean between its point of origin
(Beijing, China) and its insertion
(Seattle, U.S.). So when the father

points there and there, meaning his gallstones by
the dozens suctioned out, the boy who looks on
can almost feel his ribcage beneath him,
tender but gripping, signage says, the heart

and lungs all the harder as his young bones
strengthen for spring. Arterial trees emptied
by liquid plastic shoved up the insides
to reside a thousand years, even as a piston

moves down to let the engine take in
a cylinder-full of air and gas when
a second driver reparks the wheeled dollies
beside the tractor trailer's darkened spaces.

They say, *a donkey's lips don't fit a horse's mouth.* If I lean in for the see-through scapula spotlighted on, crated and created in its case, my own convex

spongy skull walls absorb, diffuse any impact, the cranial, occipitals, held. A dead man in bug-eyed staged surprise, his leg upthrust for the spectacle

of his last stilled soccer stunt needs at least that fiction of friction against the leather ball. *Flies never visit an egg that has no crack.* Each front axle in the moving fleet aligned true.

And can't any process occasion mishap? Once I saw something outside the baby's room glowing white-orange, gliding past the dining table into the hall and it was,

*hurry when someone's in the house* then bone zero despair, a shedding, spreading, gone. And if your fingers when reading commit maybe a four-minute fidelity to the page

we can arrest the newfound, ink incision, outfit armada, utter equator, make the further far. *Add legs to the snake after you have finished drawing it.* The bodies in chrysalis,

cardboard, wood crate, bubble wrap. *All I have done, left undone, shall do.* A dozen freight trucks spitball the city air until someone turns the key off.

## Teaching Milton on Current Events Day

Wisconsin summer through the flat steel
                pizza-oven windows wedging in,

past Gated Storage, MLK, behind
        another Dollar Plus, we're talking about

                  one of the blind seers I believe in
(*"the lake with liquid fire"*)

            as the radiator hisses hot air
                into the classroom and the students can't

                take much more of God's ways justified
      to anyone (*"His Speech, Critics*

*Say, 'Evidence-free' "*). And why should I keep
        them much longer when there's a ruckus

              of robins, blackbirds, sparrows, jays
                (*"who brings a mind not to be changed"*)

fighting over rights to the one exhaust
        funnel jutting out of the gym, when

                (*"with works of love or enmity fulfill"*)
        the kids aren't listening to one of their own

                    murmuring now about *"brooding over
the abyss,"* with the *bbhrr* and *wheeeaihy*'s

        of better squabble out there, one bird voice
butting in on the next. Today, authorities

      spoke again about the spread of evil
                among us (*". . . new and brutal details,*

sources report . . ."), and so the girl up front
in the hot pink polka-dot half-tee,

the girl (*"reinforcement we may gain*
*from hope"*) so young her real face lies hidden

beneath the still-rising dough of this one,
raises her hand (*". . . some chained by the wrists . . ."*)

to ask *isn't the enemy like Satan*
*anyway because they both change their looks*

*and location a lot, like it says right*
*here "in what shape they choose . . . can execute*

*their airy purposes.*" And I don't know
how to answer except *what do the rest*

*of you think* which is when the room vibrates
a moment with *t'weeuupp* and *rraack hoo hoo.*

But now (*"as sentencing begins in this*
*torture case"*) the boy in back with the birthmark

between his eyes that in another country
could be taken as a sign of his powers

(*"nor founded on the brittle strength of bones"*)
for vision among the dead, starts to tell

us about his friend who's home from the war.
A bullet ripped away part of this guy's

left leg and he's supposed "to be back home
two weeks for observation (*"our own loss"*)

but they're sending him back after just one
because (*"how repair"*) these days, all the men

have to be where they're needed. Last weekend
at the pool party this friend kept talking—

you know like real fast, but not *to* anyone—
he just kept talking to people who weren't

there (*a rraack a rrpb*). So when these angels
fight in heaven and it's magnificent

or whatever it can't be real or that
bad 'cause no one ends up talking to spooks

and voices and stuff or standing up
on one of those white plastic tables in his

green fatigue swimming shorts waving the pool
net at everyone screaming (*wheeeaihy*)

for them to *get down, get down now.*
Which is when the girl beside the window

starts to sob a bit and when ("*O awake,
arise or be*") the bird ("*forever fallen*")

hits the window so hard that we all turn to face
("*past mlk and gated storage*")

that damage, the stunned body on the gravel,
leaking. Which is only how the accounts

get made, if at all, in flashes ("*using
these extreme methods*"), where for a moment

we take in ("*though no new intelligence
was garnered*") a child standing on the table

in the blue pool light ("*a louder squabble
out there*"), his chest and ribs lifting like

a venetian blind in breeze as if to see
through the splices (*"disobedience and the fruit"*).

After a while the room spills forward, growing
into the boy who wants the answer now

and the other boy who answers the air
now and the air that holds the answer, but

silently now, with the bells ringing and
time to go and blood on the ground and

these voices (*"works of love"*) that are heard, that are
heard, that aren't there.

## Last Wave

No warning, the fissure, the wave, the wreck, reckoning.

No warning, mantle's woe unto trench maw, bespeaking mega thrust.

And ocean receding, fish flapping in sand, silver.

Till water curved its back, crashed, spurting stones, dogs, shards, children.

Sky, sea, two spools unwinding in wet.

Though tourists were in love, the building-sized blue arc above them.

No warning, TNT force of thirty-two billion tons.

And the father's back slapping hard, water's uppercut coming on full.

And the arms shooting open, the child let go.

And the bellow-fat beast stamping its feet unchained.

Spattering the lime-striated caves, dry a second before.

Though a woman leaps from one rooftop to another, lives.

Though in village legend, long drought follows the flood.

And the tectonic subducts drop-kick one plate against another.

Though a taxi driver pauses over his noodles at the start of thunder.

Though money's made to dance on tables, entertaining locals.

No warning, this fist, signature.

Though seafloor systems exist, pricey items.

Though boys and men run the beach, yelling *get back.*

And some bodies drag along the coral for miles.

Though one fly rubs its hands.

No warning like a voice turned inward.

Though for two hundred thousand their last taste is salt.

No warning and the voice is as if.

Sky, sea, the two spools unraveling.

The voice breaking, birthing, up-wrathed, out-wrung—

# First Child Miscarried

Out of blood bed
        and pelvic bone,
                out of the sex-shot ancient seas,

out of egg cell
        and slime maze, sperm
                trip and secret code,

you slipped from the spiral,
        saying *no*
                to the flushed luck

of lung sac, the script
        in chromosome,
                amniot slush starting up,

saying *no* to the song
        of labor and gestation,
                the hard taking form, *no*

to vein tick and flesh time,
        *no* to ancestors branching
                from the family trees:

a shoemaker in Minsk,
        a general's friend in Bangkok,
                *no* to broom-pushers in paper mills,

to lid-fitters in canneries, saying *not-to-be*
        descended from the green-eyed girl raped
                by Cossacks, from the draft dodger

of czars' armies, *no* to smithies in small villages,
  millions migrating for the sake of better
    rice pits, nomads passing over

the by-now long-sunken land bridge—
  Oh my blotch and second heart-
    beat—saying *no*

to evolution, the men come from apes come down from
  boars and frogs and lizards,
    rejecting the swill

of molecules, the cluster of microbes—
  Oh let there be no amino acids,
    let there be no first star,

saying *no*
  to the *whowhatwhenwherewhy*
    saying *no reason*—

## Drunk Tank

As salmon sidewind through
lusts of get-back-to's,
thrusting, half-annulled,

their ocean-going gills,
from fresh to salt and back
again, water rumors,

*thou shalt not stop breathing.*
Smoltification. Leaves
in a yard snap the camera

into place, nailing down one's birth
as a ready to get your mark on.
Bamboo or maple, recall,

or can't you? When what happened
takes a stance. Are classed,
actual migrations of all species—

primitive, forced, free, mass—varied
for the sake of a bet. Small fry
between par and grilse stages

grow silvery scales, coinage come
rough from hormones, cortisol,
prolactin, justice, its lack,

saying some survive better
than others. Once, not sober,
I didn't care, much, the 911'd ones

knocking, that vaporing under.
Everyone thumb-
tacked to the episode and the slim

gray second after. Change starts
with my mother, face lacing up
its insides, mirror-sick, her fourteen-

hour flight culminating in
collapse from the land of.
Push, pull factors,

the traffic human, Goths and Visis
Vandals, Vikings, Moors, landings
on Mars. One fish forfeits,

fins blacken. As for the call
beneath your answering, you
would crawl to get there.

# Motherland

*(after Robert Hayden)*

*The Amsterdam, The Angel, The Dauphin, The Phoenix*

    Merchant ships anchored at the river mouth
        sails hung like
             bedsheets after a night of sweat

West to East and back again, we travel in trade of the skin

    "For their use in place of leather, my Lord,
    whole cargo holds of deer pelt and dried ray,
    the profit free of duty."

                    *The Charlotte, The Globe, The Hopewell,*
                    *The Hound, The Kristian, The Good Consent*

    Girls brought across the border, held down
    in "the room for unveiling of virgins"

Also the rudderless byways, the years'
        tide swell slap at one water bank

    *O but I shall not want*        *Equipped Lord for every good work*

And when the plot stutters forward        in circles,   in circus,   in yes sirs

    "The ship loaded with silk and rare honey
    young boys adept at the arts of love
    plus two baby elephants bound for His Majesty"

                    *The Land of Smiles, The Personal Service,*
                    *The Patent Massage, The Sex Tour*

Later one shape, a slope in the mud,
        this contour becoming chronicle
                this history set in stone

        More than 500,000 in U.S. troops stationed, in need of R&R

                        *The Maiden Tribute, The Modern Babylon,*
                        *The Millions of Bodies, The Golden Maze*


And according to a neighbor the girl called "Lek," meaning "little,"
was sold at age three to the foreign businessman

                A wolf speaks, while chewing
                the lamb,
                        "I can say quite clearly that
                        I do not see anything wrong with my desires"

For the family owed a great debt and the father could not work

                        "I believe
                        many children know just what they want"

                        *The Lord is my helper*

        "She watched while the neighbor was paid
        to masturbate him. A few weeks later Lek did
        the same and continued to do so until she began,
        at the age of six, to have intercourse with her owner."

                        *That through Him all men might believe*

        "Sending bombardiers and blunderbusses
        His Majesty has resolved to attack,
        to become its master by force of arms."

                        *The Lord is my helper I shall not be afraid*

Each of the girls wears a number
         as she dances before the mirror

                    Meantime
                    Now
                    In between
                    Then
                    One
                    Shape
                    Not
                    Another
                    XX
                    Not
                    XY
                    Get the picture
                    Forget the picture
                    Meantime


              "If
              I could choose
              I would take just one girl
              I would love her with all my heart"

Number 42 steps forward, shakes

         *Even angels long to look     equipped for every good work*

The TV always on and I remember

         Mother singing *I am*
                    *Siamese if you please*

As if we could step off the stutter

                         *Bless The Globe, The Hopewell, The Good*
                *Consent*

Plus boners for billboard faces
The secret cash-cunt deposit that's
Sony'd, Toshiba'd, IMF'd, IBM'd

*There by the grace of*

The body wholly body, spirit eaten out
We travel in trade
We owe a great debt

There is no speaking for here
Though there is singing

*"entrusting our souls to the limitless sea"*

Then and now now and then
the profit free of duty
the vessels unveiled in the harbor

heavy with rubies, emeralds, diamonds,
buying honey and moonlight,
waves on the wood planks shushing, slapping,

the child praying
*I shall not be afraid*
*I shall not be*

## The Rumor of Evolution

                    Spare a thought for infinity's fat plonk.
        Theory of bang, conjecture of whoop,
crack and fall pushing past
              the wit's forever prior to.

    Think heat but not
as hot as it once was. Some of the dust
          spit raveling to planets,
                  some of the cores cooling to moons.

As for the after-party, we've got the pictures:
          a little plasma of becoming,
                  a spun-violent banquet swirling out.

Though "high temperatures erase
          all memory of early states"
              the young still-yolky stars
                 look blue lit as frozen snow.

And if there's one thing we know,
          it's Form
              as we know it. From
plovers to mountains to pickup trucks,

                        everything gets
         sprouted from the stellar dirt and wild
                detritus
               slowing
                   down.

In size, more
        zeroes than the mind can hold.
                Not to mention the No

Getting Around,
by now, our imagining everything
as if
the As of
Us.

Also, "reason thus
enters the scene
in place of understanding."

Somewhere else a voice saying
speak, don't speak.
Later too, ocean's spat
with sky ongoing, the puny $H_2Os$
shuttling back and forth.

Then the come-ons:
mold and weeds,
starter shoots, fin and fowl, sunken
clouds, the lesser
sticker fish.

Plus one ape backlit
by lightning and
a second
forked creature who runs away,

which is to say:

arrives a single sword to cleave earth from the heavens.

As hallowed be thy universal laws one-upping it all,
the strong force
(matter held together),
the weak force
(atoms pulled apart).

Oh but you can't hear it anymore, the voice having spoken:
  some folded of cortex,
                some flat in the forehead, sloped.
After a while "race based on appearance
                being too crude for biology" largely
ignored.

        By which it was pronounced:
          a few tooled cerebral,
              others just eddies in the skull, typeset.

                Giving us, at the end of each single stem,

brain's hills and valleys, our three-pound
        home in the head, solid
              as an egg, hard-boiled.

                        Afloat in its little bath of seawater,
          coddled with ganglia, nerve endings, descended to
the wondrous
        so-called uncus.

                Also someone told us
      to question the question, mumbling
at one another on the long spectrum:

          *soul, self, separate, sidereal, sidelong, sex*

    Given: a spank of mind over matter looking like
        the cattle all ours,
              quartered in barns.
    Given: "organisms unequipped
        to generate core
              consciousness
                are condemned . . ."

35

Meanwhile, the cities planted, root bulb
after root bulb breaking the land. Blooming
emperors and rent boys,
steam engines and water closets,
arsenals, smallpox, art . . .

". . . to making images of sight or sound or touch . . ."

Building slums and H-bombs, cloverleafs and capitals

". . . but they cannot come to know what they did"

Until it's after the need of god it's another force granting

*as fronds of rockweed dangle across the rock*

". . . the army . . . must be agile, and lethal . . . readily deployable . . ."

*as colored holdfasts*
*in the base, buoyed*
*by air-filled bladders*

". . . require a minimum of logistical support
as the battle may go on indefinitely . . ."

*a rising and swaying*
*with ocean surge, ridden,*
*the waters flowing over,*
*the small periwinkles feeding*

*every which way they can—*

# Then

*(a second pregnancy)*

First to let him in. Spasm
                  that starts invisibles under the skin.

Our motion that uncovers motion.

Then a missing wire in the chain link, feeling it.
To find out by

        the lines / no lines changing our lives.
                    Six-dollar drugstore device.

Be
        that as it may, a cloud
                bud's been pinched off,
        winched out the other side.

Meanwhile waves of sickness prickle the I of I, erasing.
Next all
        throat-to-gut muttering
                pain, the lava-to-saliva mutinies, more revs
                    revving up the chest tube.

For instance, the flesh has two gates. Enters the one not seen.

And so there must be soreness in spots
        ordinarily ignored,
                tonsil, jaw,
                    stomach palate's tender underside.

    Little core
        simply to be.
        Any smell wild strong.

Cook in this house and I'll kill you.
You reek of cantaloupe.
I'm not complaining. OK I'm . . .

A change in perspective,
seeing all that collects in the bowl's back rim.

To be told it won't last.
Cancel any task that can be.

Exists: nothing
and the nothing else.

Then in the clearing of nausea—gripping ellipsis—to start to feel him bit by bit,
the baby, a blood-mucus'd cherry stone
muscling up to your muscle.

Notched in time.
Still *pre-*, but *due.*
And how the world sets out to
world him as you were: recompense.

Or to remember yourself young, the morning's thrill waking up,
eating maple syrup on new snow,
icy sweet, infinite

desire, those days, before
the long-ruled
cinch into law.

Which is to say who says
it wants to come down, get born, sit
at the table of simmering?
Oh better beneath
the belly's tent, in prelim tissue,
gentle
placental
swim.

Though the body, once started,
    tends unstoppable,
        hitched to the calendar's tear-away
            cliffs.

While we are we, two mouths, heartbeats,
    four eyes opening, closing,
    four fists in sleep-twitch.

    And beneath the ultra-
sound slop, the inked-in TV screen sheds
        firsts of you,
        herks and jerks of you.

Are you ready?
Nothing left to do but panic.

        Has two gates, entering by one.

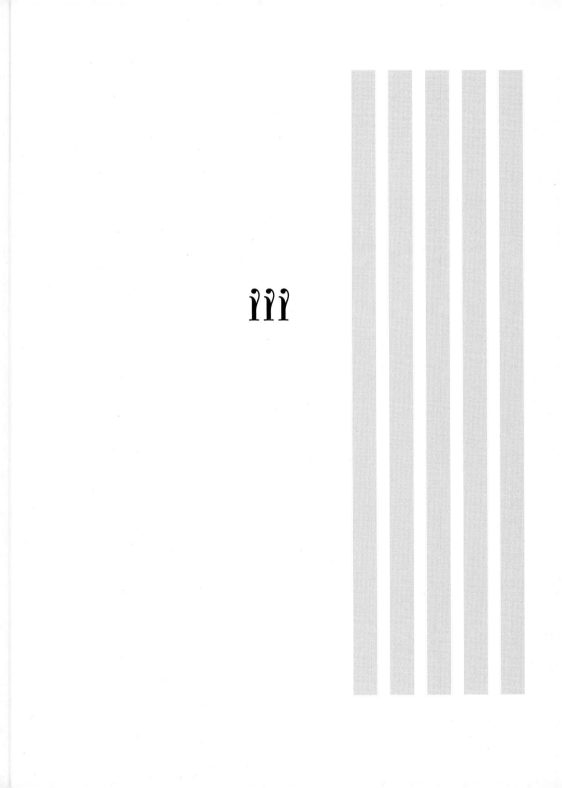

## Birth Event

So how will he come, new-flanged,
　　　　　out of the balm and starry
mic-mac, out of ducal
　　　　　　　mansions and astral melt

　　　　　　　　　　　　　　*Rapid, the dividing,*
　　　　*time torn to his first*
　　　　　　　　　　　*instant.　　　As in shiver,*
　　　*the fast coming upon*

Ah, give me my own
　　　　　celestial ingot,
zigzag angel, arriving,
　　　　　　crying his dictums of spurn and glee

　　　　　　　　　　　　　*The innards'*
　　　*uncontrollable*
　　　　　　　*roll of boulders.*
　　　　　　　　　　　　　　*As on this day a sword shall*
　　　*unsuture your soul*

With eyes cinctured diamond,
his hands a galactic
　　　　　　mélange that can grasp,
the small nails, just cloven

　　　　　　　　　　　*Pain has a plan*
　　　*to say more so.*

*Cleaving*

                      *forceps to unfold the fold*

And afterwards, how
         did he get here,

             crowning my roundness,
sleeping still feral, finical, nursing always

                          *For he eats you open*
              *from the inside.*

Having to cult us over,
         kneel us down to his lymph nodes,
            halo'd, hallowed,
               appetited by heft

                      *Some breeds of death barking*
        *not far behind:*
              *what I was, could*
                   *have been,*

A new voice, outside me, of a sudden.
        Owning his own. Until
what is he now,

                *what he was, might*
      *have*
             *been*

sleeping,
        waking, bubbled, bodied up,
           this being

                  *the might-not-have-been*
      *of him*

Until who is
a whom so new, this now and now,
        each second I look down

                *if*

                        *not*
        *for the knot*

                *of him, becoming*

his all and only,
        two wild blues beseeching

# The Rumor of Myth

*(Thetis on Achilles, the son)*

Starts in estuary
> whelm and whirl of rock-skin,
sea-swell, the hove called salt.
> I loved
the hero-to-be,
> his life first arrowed unto me,

> > scudding, spared, still
> > unconscious.

> No
> > *he* and *she* to wash
> away yet, my
inhale planked to his ex—.
> > Plus our everywhere-wet
> > trough
> > > in the tidal
> waves repeating
> > over and over.

Given, milky teats, realm of belly,
given, his body my body by faith.

Which to keep him I'd
> cozen, always,
guarding every
> waterway I owned.

See hand, heart, heel
> > where I dipped him, to save.

See the would-be bargain,
                              back ridge of epic,

hovering in half-truths as if I really could
                              unwick what was to come.

In the end when they took him
                    the spell of the world sang
          *name, rank, date*
of birth, your mother's
                              maiden, your father's post.

Still, I said *no hands*

                              *out the window, boy,*
          I said *no swimming*

                              *at the water's edge.*

          *Sand's oozy blank's where they've got oblivion, boy,*

          *so listen you get back here right now.*

          Nothing worked. He wanted all the wrong
                              toys, tanker's prow,
the true-edged sword, a golden set of spears.

          And when it came to the armor, god-hammered, bronze
through the beam,

                              well, I never begged. Another
                    exoskeleton, extra
skull. Though I'd made him perfect, zodiac'd
                    to last.

                    Meanwhile, time being,
          on that outline-horizon,
                              you could see empire

serrated at the edges: junk boats,

                                    great ships,

the soldiers waving, even the geese
                defined in Vs.


                      Soon each new sight needled.
         And Fame, that bitch, stuck

like a splinter inside him,
                    cutting the flesh

in whispers, rumoring,
        *you can win, you can win.*
            Wood hewn like a beast at the door.

# The Body in Three Acts

1

## Porn

Visceral, her kick pleat in aspic—
    gamy, full swank.
Then cocks on the gallows,
    then you can't take your eyes off

this hinterland, where once upon the first,
    not to mention mythic, time
she saw his mainmast go
    at a gallop and ah,

it was good. Meanwhile, the girl
    all whirly
on her pile of dildos. Sure, teenage
    at the time, much unctuous

prelude until we had our own
    jibe and tussle
to get the thing done. Then came
    the furloughing

each to each wherein someone
    discovers his singular
disgust. Finding, perhaps,
    a soul-part frostbit,

bare as one thumb laid down
    in the pee-stained snow.
Banished. Still, after a while,
    someone always says, let's do it again.

**Thai Sex Tour**

Comes, our tourist, by far and by fang,
his newfangled regalia paid for.

His first stint by way of brothel, seeking
a cure for the lady cruel, the she who ill'd him

something awful. If hoping, as promised,
what happens stays, then all the better,

as this or that woman bends
from the bodice incessant. Oh but she's heard

of Sheboygan and wants to go there. This game
to get out of, a long twist 'til the frigid

just bray and wiggle. Who wants to know
when lust swallowed the all and sundry?

Who gets how scurvy hit her country,
curving her history ever? As if his past,

ungettable at, could explain him. Searching for
new coupling itself, gone cleaner, more animus,

less hampered by sweat and nougat. Alas, so little
to hand-hold, this quiver that keeps us. And anyone

can say: blighted, the self, or some of it,
coming cloven to begin with. Anyone feels

how the powers that be vaguely brine up
whatever big justice there was.

## 3

## Child

As before this, nothing but an abacus of until's.

Then a cervix thinning, letting you tunnel unto

the bandaged days. The you that's you—

in, already—one irresistible body built

to resist. Small wonder the birth of trust comes,

publishing your gazettes of night cries, unthumbed.

Gamboling, we stumble. For the inscrutable news,

your story, still breaking, to stun.


Go ahead, wail out what's left, remembering, maybe,

an elsewhere's not-to-be-faulted spheres.

Give us the uncut chords.

I carried the score for you to be.

Footprints on my insides, clear.

Listening now, beyond heard, to your prodigious unword.

# The House of Rumor

## 1. /As/Of

After the apogee of appetite.
After the boys drop-kicking a cow skull all down the street.
After cousin'd to credences, these.
After the dog they hung for the witch who wanted.
After an eye for an eye, the enemy agents.
After feathers on the bike trail beside the fresh blood.
After gossip turned into gospel.
After the sheep heart in the parking lot stuck with rose thorns.
After the improvised news.
After the jokes about how many lightbulbs.
After knowledge storming the storm.
After lying inside a man, a thousand thoughts he can't know.
After memory began to mutter.
After nightly they checked on him sleeping.
After offal was found in the driveway.
After proof rounded the corner called hearsay.
After quitting the seventh son of the seventh.
After reports of riots, strains run amok.
After splicing the slave ships into ads for eye candy.
After the tea party ended, a gulping of millions.
After underground streams bilged up the one god singing.
After the vixen besmudged the headwaiter.
After water broke through water.
After xeroxing the blessed virgin.
After you beat I by a hair.
After zeniths crashing to contain.

## 2. What You Really Need Is

To hear he is breathing for certain.
If so      If so      If
Not
If not in innocence
In where
Is he
A place
Is he placed
If not here, where
Is he      he is
is he not
is he not whose
is this      still he is
gaining     touch

and come down
for the tongue in-
tended for him


## 3. If the Tongue Is a Door

*labiodental*
snails us sacramental
leaving lab rats in entrails,
dear *labiodental*

*coronal*'s
a boner, a fine-time first stoner,
four star all-aloner, please don't
heckle the folks bespeaking *coronal*

*alveolar,*
come as you are, it needn't be
far, this tongue's looking to spar,
ah give it a rest, *alveolar*

*retroflex*
plus wheat chex
equals whatever's best, the next
is next, the road taken, *retroflex*

*apical's*
gone radical, spectacular
and macular, oh that topical
stuff just doesn't work

Back again, back again, close the door softly.


## 4. More from the Conquered City

"Whenever there was a pause in the bomb-
ing and shelling, everyone went out in
search of food and fuel. At the beginning,
one shop was still open, selling just one
item: "pudding powder" for making the
gelatin dessert blancmange. But other-
wise people simply appropriated
anything edible they could see—
including nettles. There were plenty of
those growing on bombed sites, and when
there was a bit of gas in the stove we
made nettle soup. It took forever, because
the gas pressure was so feeble. Then the
gas stopped altogether, and the elec-
tricity as well. When the radio
stopped too, all news became hearsay . . ."

## 5. Ovid's Tabloid

At the world's INSIDE center is a place
between the land and seas and E! and the
celestial regions, where the tripartite
universe is joined with Brad's Fears Over
Baby, and from this point everything that's
anywhere, like the Awful Truth (no matter
how far off) can be observed by Liz
Taylor's Secret Love Child
and every voice goes right into its ears.
                         Rumor lives here beside
*The National Enquirer*; she chose
this house herself, well situated on
a mountaintop, near Paris' Simple
Life, adding some features of her own
like a Daily Box Office and it has
innumerable entrances and a
thousand apertures—so The Boogeyman
Comes Out of the Closet but not one door;
by day and night it lies completely open,
clicking Hot Gossip under Party Crash.
          It is constructed of resounding brass,
A Glam Crowd that murmurs constantly as
A High Priestess Tells Us Weekly, carrying
back all that it hears, How to Make Your Own
Voodoo Doll & Watch Your Troubles Disappear!
which it reiterates; there is no quiet
anywhere within, and when Stars Take to
the Air, not a part of it is free from
noise; no clamor here, just whispered murmurings
until Everyone's Grassy Knolling About
the ocean heard from far away . . .

## 6. Conception

So once I asked him whether he would
live his life again, and I meant
moment by moment without
any knowledge of doing it again, just to
live through again if he could, exactly
the same, and he said
no. Then why make another

## 7. Ovid's Tabloid (cont'd)

Crowds fill
the entryway, a fickle mob In the News
that comes and goes; and rumors everywhere,
thousands of Press Leaks, of fabrications
mixed with fact, while Would-Be Weapons Do
Damage wandering the premises and
false reports flit all about, as U.S.
Citizens May Be Handed Over and
some fill their idle ears with others' words,
and some go bearing tales, named Intelligence,
and everywhere the Millions Protest Cartoons,
while fictions grow, as everyone adds on
Despite Howls to what he's heard. Here are
Credulity and Heedless Error,
as NATO Troops Fire with Empty Joy
and Fearful Consternation; and here is
What the Chief of Staff Knew with Unexpected
Treachery, Whisperers of Uncertain
Origin; nothing that happens, Eight Killed

in Bombing, whether here on earth or in
the heavens or seas below, is missed, On-
lookers Are Shot as information leaks an age.


## 8. Telephone Game

"Empire waists are in this season."
"Choirs of heartache forgo the reason."
"Such dire straits, prison bars for treason."
"Desire quakes a cigar's secretion."
"They conspired to break into the czar's meeting."
"He berated the cause as far too queasy."

> *The network extends worldwide,*
> *so you can reach nearly anyone*
> *on the planet. When you compare that*
> *to the state of the world just 100 years ago,*
> *you realize how amazing the phone is!*


"These liars are great in bars for teasing."
"Some wild mistakes demand completion."
"Inspired apes can guard accretion."
"Spitfires make a war of bleeding."
"Expired cupcakes are increasing."
"Tired rump flakes roar obscenely."

> *Any "real" telephone contains a device*
> *called a duplex coil or something*
> *equivalent to block the sound of your own*
> *voice from reaching your own ear.*

## 9. Present

Here's the lake we live beside
for your sake changing so it looks like
pavement then gray shag carpet sun-sequined
then pewter'd dust from a summer plum if no
version stays then what are you when you say
"hole" when you say "rock" you are trying
hard to be like the world


## 10. To Whom It May Concern

Nightly, we check on him sleeping.
To hear he is breathing for certain.
We close the door slowly.

After the asking, gratitude.
The air in, the air out,
making a soft sound.

## Abstract and Figure

(Persephone Unbound *and* Perre's Ventaglio III,
*Beverly Pepper, Olympic Sculpture Park, Seattle)*

Betimes, the hunt scuttled again,
a child upthrust in rock. Follow

the belows it knows of: ground
cover, pinnate frond, withering bitter-

root there to mask, no, mark the brute
clearing. Some force having

fretted over the ever-
about-to-be-snatched-

again stillness. (*You left me
in the open field.*) Further,

the land scaped
past its long-ago

use by wanderers, once free to build
fires. Before that, totems beside

the Sound so a people could
take their place. Glacier slice. Pliocene.

A great rain trumping on the yawed
caldera. (*I said I would be right*

*back.*) As if we can enter by
polished steel that mirrors the half-

dozen thunderhead anvils
this one sky comes down to.

Now just look at what she's done,
her bronze midsection tethered,

textured, tongued until
what light there is resurfaces

as world squared
empty, squared full.

# Three Plays on Display

1

**Ultrasound**

My Dearest, my soon-      to-be citizen:      these are the made things.
    Today's      bounce back,      the inked-in sound waves
        showing your face spun shadows, ten digits' skeletal glow—

version of version      to us, outside,
    nurse-allowed,      kindly M.D.—coaxed:
        your heartbeat a four-square backlit jellyfish.


    Ambassador      pulsing      from a far sea.

Soon you'll see, this side,      how technique      forges, forces
    the assorted, the all.      We get ghost photos
      icicled.      Your sac of shore

    encroaching, your brain budding its someday sputter of *I,I,I,I.*

Our vision      of you
    in grainy swill      your nation      black/blood/eggplant
      pledged to the camera's

    slide, its tale to tell—*erase new view erase.*


I can tell you this,      if you ask in time
    what was my face      before      I was born,
      love,      the story's

never stable. You were,      are,      motion,
    a wave below      the wave      that you can change
      as this world changes you.

61

## American Museum of Natural History, New York

So getting back to Jumbo the Elephant,
        this is how he jumped
                the tracks, but badly.

The Floating Waters, The Ancient Apes, The Prehistorics, The Insect Wing

        At home and abroad the interrogators
        are tired of limelight.

The great giant having escaped, you see,
        from P. T. Barnum,
           then run down
                by the railroad train.

*This is the way we wash our hands, wash our hands*

The metropolis, the affronted, the spiky, the columnar, the plinth

        "There is a need for permanence
        in the heart of the city,
        a restoration of origin."

Thus Jumbo, now stuffed, preens, drowses, at once.
        Pure beast to see, sans serif.
        Hooded, leathern, astral eyes.

Nouns being in this game: Nature. Primitive. Other.
                Also: Gnat. Primate. Mother.

Children file by, unriled, to look.

Because necropolis, nest of cement, internetted, interspersed.
       Given much huffing and hunting, this,
              the bodies appearing,
                     images taking us.

The photos, the bagged head, the FlexiCuffs.
       The men piled naked, the girl's thumbs-up.

5,442 kg gray African male, 6 years of age, 1.56 meter tusk

Whose America, which display?
       The boot to the neck, the prolonged exposure, the panties over their faces.

           "To enter the Roosevelt Wing
           you must pass through Teddy well mounted
           as father and protector
           between Indian and African,
           both standing,
           dressed as 'savages.' "

*This is the way we wash our hands, wash our hands, so*

The stress positions, the darker
       necessities,
              the epic adventure

       *early in the morning*

Child,
       still water-lung'd
            covered in fur,
                 swaddled in belly mud, ooze, you'll be made
                 to look.

## 3

## National Museum of Culture, Thailand

August dark, druid dark, flesh of your flesh.
The case, that is, the world, behind cases. Anciently splayed

umbrellas in beryl, in amber. A woman burning,
                    claw-nailed, behind her trellis of gold.

Verbs being, my love: to culture, to build, to accrue. Also,
            to cult, to buy, to rue. Yours to inherit,

                    the dark halls elephantine chariots
of kings, the silver headdress sown mother-of-pearl,

gold stupas holding up the temple by teardrop.
            Regarding this minute, this space

you're bred into, you have to take it, back room and all, past
                    minaret plate glass and tea sets,

            lacquered trays and teak barges
pleated in filigree, flesh of your flesh.

                    Here's a plaque for your great-grandfather.
His photo, dust-embalmed,

                    would-be revolutionary,
one of the winners for a moment, buttoned

bronze, wanting to be modern, which is to say, like us.
            We come from colonels

and field marshals, small-time city officials, running
            the muck of corruptions. As for debris

this side of history, it's yours. Once,
outside these doors, the student uprisings started,

the seventy-seven shot dead on cement, this flesh,
that flesh, yours. In the name of democracy, in the name

of the clean, the soldiers' blood-and-smoke
ate its way from AK-47s. Until

today in the street, standing traffic
choke holds the city, spews

the scene—white and green taximeters, pickups
hauling kids to the factories, the families surgical-

masked, piled three and four to a moped.
Yours, that monk who's in hiding, waiting for a bus. I can tell you

he's one of our relations, exiled, a rigger of fake state lotteries.
Or I can give you the aunt, her face fallen as if filled with sand,

her supper brought in on a tray, the twenty-two
tiny bowls of what she won't throw away, week-old

noodles, mangosteens shriveled in brine, my lovely,
my child, flesh of my flesh. Also the one-legged girl

begging before the 7-Eleven, the one whose parents
had to maim her

so she could make a better living. Oh please, look up,
look out. Past the scrambled-egg trees, the toad-

squatted gray business buildings, past the chiffon-
topped houses of prayer. Rumor has it, the flesh of your

flesh has no need
to keep you. It's the same sky. Same swallows

on their way home to nest. Dear born-to,
skin of my skin, do what you can

with your turn—
speak the world, let it go.

# acknowledgments

Grateful acknowledgment goes to the editors of the following journals
in which several of these poems first appeared: *American Literary Review,
Canary, Ploughshares,* and *TriQuarterly.*

For constant support, creative and otherwise, deepest love to Andrew
Feld. Enormous gratitude to Martha Collins, whose artistic insight and
scrupulous attention gave the book its final arc. And huge appreciation to
those friends who read the manuscript and were so generous with their
time, care, and suggestions: Edward Hirsch, Corey Marks, and Heather
McHugh. Many thanks to Mike Levine for making it happen. Lastly, love
and thanks to Nick Twemlow, who inspired with editorial vision, friendship,
and faith, and who always let me talk it through.

# notes

The epigraph is from Ovid, *Metamorphoses*, trans. Charles Martin (New York: Norton, 2004), 409.

### Family Spirits, with Voice of One Child Miscarried

The voice of the unborn spirit enters in the traditional Thai form of *khap yanii.* In it each line is broken into two parts consisting of five and six syllables each. The fifth syllable must rhyme with the eighth syllable of the first line. The last syllable of the first line must also rhyme with the fifth of the second, while the second line's final syllable must rhyme again with the last syllable of the third line, and so on, repeating the internal fifth and eighth syllable pattern as well.

### The Rumor of Necessity

This poem is dedicated to Robyn Schiff. Warm thanks also to Alan Williamson, who inspired.

### *Bodies, the Exhibition,* Last Day with Ancient Sayings

Several details are based on the exhibition that appeared in many American cities showcasing preserved bodies dissected to display bodily systems. Some of the italicized lines are ancient Asian proverbs. Thanks go to Brad Harvey.

### Teaching Milton on Current Events Day

This poem is dedicated to Susan Mitchell. Several of the italicized phrases are taken from the following: John Milton, *Paradise Lost,* Book I (New York: Penguin Books, 1981); Michael Kranish and Bryan Bender, "Bush Backs Cheney on Assertion Linking Hussein, Al Qaeda," *Boston Globe,* June 16, 2004; Mark Danner, "The Logic of Torture," *New York Review of Books,* vol. 51, no. 11, June 24, 2004.

**Motherland**

Some details were inspired by Dirk van der Cruysse, *Louis XIV et le Siam* (Chiang Mai, Thailand: Silkworm Books, 2002); and Jeremy Seabrook, *Travels in the Skin Trade* (London: Pluto, 2001). A few phrases from the New Testament also appear.

**The Rumor of Evolution**

Various quotations, somewhat altered, are taken from the following sources: John D. Barrow, *The Artful Universe* (New York: Back Bay Books, 1996); Jean-François Lyotard, *Lessons on the Analytic of the Sublime* (Palo Alto, Calif.: Stanford University Press, 1994); Steve Olson, *Mapping Human History* (Boston: Mariner Books, 2003); Antonio Damasio, *The Feeling of What Happens* (New York: Harvest Books, 2000); Peter J. Boyer, "A Different War," *New Yorker*, July 1, 2002, 54; and Jennifer L. Ackerman, *The Curious Naturalist* (Washington, D.C.: National Geographic, 1998).

**The House of Rumor**

Section 4 is from Gabriele Annan, "When the Russians Came," review of *A Woman in Berlin: Eight Weeks in the Conquered City*, by Anonymous, *New York Review of Books*, vol. 52, no. 15, October 6, 2005. Sections 5 and 7 borrow from Ovid, *Metamorphoses*, Book XII, trans. Charles Martin (New York: Norton, 2004). Section 8 features a few phrases from http://www.communication.howstuffworks.com, a Web page that discusses the uses and history of the telephone.

**Abstract and Figure**

During the writing of this poem, I had in mind two statements by Beverly Pepper, which appear beside her work. The first is: "The abstract language of form that I have chosen has become a way to explore an interior life of feeling . . . I wish to make an object that has a powerful presence, but is at the same time inwardly turned, seeming capable of intense self-absorption." The second is: "Stainless steel, polished to a mirror finish.

The idea is that from whatever angle you view it, the voids seem filled and the solids seem empty."

**Three Plays on Display**

Section 2: Phrases in quotation marks are adapted from Donna Haraway, *Primate Visions* (New York: Routledge, 1989), 26–27.

# about the author

Pimone Triplett is the author of two previous collections of poetry, *The Price of Light* and *Ruining the Picture*, and the coeditor of an anthology of essays, *Poet's Work, Poet's Play*. She is an associate professor in the creative writing program at the University of Washington.